This book is a moving emotional story to bless and strengthen family relationships. A love story regarding parent-child relationship, spouse communication, and having a strong emphasis motivating toward personal growth in trusting God. The reading of this book will help shape a positive self-image of family values when today our family has been severely challenged. Don't miss the blessing of this book. You will be inspired to daily express love for family members

Rev. Robert "Bob" L. Deaton

. . . .

This is a story that touches the soul and brings joy to the heart of its reader. As the story unfolds, we are made aware of how God is always with us in our life's journey and how He still answers prayers.

I have been Troy Webster's pastor for the past fourteen years and consider it a privilege to be a friend of the man of faith. You will be blessed by his writing.

Robert Bevill, Pastor, Poplar Springs Baptist Church

Hey Mister

TROY WEBSTER

CROSS BOOKS

CrossBooks™
1663 Liberty Drive
Bloomington, IN 47403
www.crossbooks.com
Phone: 1-866-879-0502

First published by CrossBooks 11/23/2009

ISBN: 978-1-6150-7050-3 (sc)

Library of Congress Control Number: 2009940130

*Printed in the United States of America
Bloomington, Indiana*

This book is printed on acid-free paper.

DEDICATION

This book is dedicated to Carolyn Webster my beloved wife and dearest friend. I have been so blessed to know her as a wife, mother, grandmother and great grandmother. Our family has been truly blessed by her faith, love and prayers. She is the strong, yet gentle thread that knits the fibers of our family together. Beautiful reflections of her and here love are lived out in them every day. As my wife of fifty-six years, I will never comprehend how I have been so blessed to have her in my life. She is my continued answered prayer.

Special thanks to Larry Ross for editing.

Illustrations are by Bill McNeely

Contents

INTRODUCTION

This is a story of redemption, Christian love and family ties. The story is about average people, the trials and opportunities they face, and the importance of trusting in God to lead along life's path.

The characters, like all humans, are not perfect, but realize their needs and trust in God to meet those needs.

A little boy touches the heart of the adults in the story and a great truth from his past confronts Dale Goodman. His bride is reluctant to embrace the child, but comes to love him and accept him into their home.

In the end, God blesses this family in a special way and rewards them with something that has been one of their fondest wishes.

CHAPTER 1

The Early Years

$\mathcal{D}$ale Goodman graduated from the University of Alabama in 1970, on a Thursday. They had a farewell party that night. The party turned out to be wild and he wasn't sure that he remembered everything that happened. On Friday morning he and his roommate packed their clothes and headed home to Greensboro, NC. His roommate, Joe, was riding with him and he dropped him off in Atlanta Ga. Dale thought, "Joe is a fun guy. He is always the life of the party. Rooming together for four years was great and he's a great friend. We always had fun at all of the parties and doing all the things that college guys do. I know he'll be practicing law in Atlanta, but we need to keep in touch."

Dale reached Greensboro late Friday night and was sure glad to be home.

Dale had sent out several resumes and had an interview on Tuesday. He spent the weekend with family and friends.

He went for the interview on Tuesday with a law firm in Greensboro. It wasn't the biggest firm, but he thought this would give him the experience he needed. They offered him the job, and he went to work on Monday morning.

Dale had some very interesting cases and eventually earned a good reputation. Dale was happy in his work, but his personal life wasn't what he wanted it to be.

He was a very handsome man, six feet tall, blonde hair and blue eyes. He dated several girls, but never seemed to find the one he wanted to spend his life with. He knew it was time for him to settle down and have a family, but he was still living with his parents.

He met Nancy Adair, who had finished high school with him. Nancy was a very attractive and petite girl with black hair and brown eyes. She had gone to college and had become a registered nurse at a local hospital.

Dale asked her out for lunch. They had a nice lunch and talked about high school days. Most of their friends were already married. She asked why Dale hadn't married, and he told her, "I did get married. It was while I was in college and to a girl I thought really loved me. I found out later that she didn't".

He continued, "After about a month, she decided that she didn't want to be married, so she called her dad to come and get her. He had the marriage annulled, and I never saw her again.

When Dale asked Nancy why she hadn't married, she said, "Well, the right man never came along".

Dale said, "I found out one thing. You never know what is in a person's heart. When the right person comes along, I plan to marry again".

Nancy said, "I'm sorry things turned out like they did for you. I have to go for now, but maybe you can go to church with me sometime."

Dale said, "I never did care for that church stuff".

Nancy replied, "Maybe that is part of your problem. I remember when you and your family used to go to church."

"That was a long time ago, and a lot of things have happened since then."

As they walked to her car, Nancy said, "Dale, maybe we could have lunch again sometime and talk some more."

As they walked, Dale thought," I really enjoyed having lunch with Nancy. She is a very intelligent girl, and I would like to see her again."

Dale had to go out of town for a few days, but he decided he would call her when he got back into town. He was back on Friday, and called Nancy to ask her to dinner on Saturday and a movie of her choosing. She was working Saturday evening, but thought the next Saturday would be good. Dale called that Friday to confirm their date.

They went to Nancy's favorite restaurant and a movie. They had a great time. Nancy had a bubbly personality that was very appealing to Dale. She was interested in some of the cases that he had tried, and shared many of her work experiences with him as well.

CHAPTER 2

Dale is Saved

couple of weeks went by and Dale thought a lot about the things Nancy had said. He called her and asked her to have lunch again. She agreed to meet on Saturday.

They had a nice lunch and decided to go somewhere quieter to talk. They went to a nearby park where they had played as kids. They enjoyed going back to the park.

After a while, Nancy said, "Dale I like you, but I don't think we should get too close because I am a Christian. I believe what the Bible says about being unequally yoked. I want to marry and have a Christian home. You know that I come from a large family and I want several children of my own."

Dale said, "I want several children of my own, too. I did enjoy going to church when I was young."

Nancy said, "I would like to see you become a Christian. Would you like to carry me to church tomorrow?"

Dale nodded and replied, "Yes, I would. I enjoy my job and being home with my family, but my life seems empty."

"Dale, Christ can fill that empty place in your life. I have to go now, but you know where I live and can pick me up at 10:30 in the morning."

They walked back to their cars, Dale hugged her, and that was the first time that they had touched. He said, "I will see you in the morning".

When he got in his car, he thought, "I really like her, but I don't want her to know it. I don't feel I am worthy of her. I have known her family all my life and I don't think I could fit into her Christian family."

Dale picked her up the next morning and they went to church. They sang many of the old hymns, and it seemed as if the preacher spoke straight to him. He enjoyed the service and saw many people he had known for a long time. They invited him to come back to church.

When they gave the invitation, Dale had the urge to go down and talk to the pastor. He felt that he wanted to accept Christ, but didn't know how.

He carried Nancy out for lunch and afterwards, carried her home. He told her that he really enjoyed the service. She asked if he would like to go back to the night service.

Dale replied, "I sure would. I think I have some unfinished business there".

They went back to church on Sunday night and during the invitation, Nancy turned and asked Dale if he would like to acknowledge Jesus Christ as his Savior?

He responded, "Yes", and asked, "Will you go forward with me to talk to the pastor? The pastor knew Nancy. He spoke to both of them and asked Dale if he wanted to join the church.

Dale said, "No, I want to become a Christian. The pastor read the plan of salvation from the Bible. Dale accepted the Lord as his Savior. He had never felt so good in his entire life.

Both Dale and Nancy were crying by now, and Dale told the pastor, "Now I want to join the church".

When they left the church, they went by Dale's parents to tell them he had been saved. His mom and dad were very happy.

Dale carried Nancy home. He told her that since he had carried her out to lunch and to church, now he was asking for a date.

"I think that can be arranged," she said with a smile.

They dated a few times and seemed to hit it off immediately. They both wanted the same things out of life, including professional careers. They both came from large families, and each wanted children. After much prayer, they felt they were meant for each other.

CHAPTER 3

Dale and Nancy are Married

After dating through the summer and meeting each other's family, Dale and Nancy decided to set a wedding date. They selected a date and a time that would be convenient for both of their families and work schedules. Their employers gave them a week off for the wedding. They went on a trip to Jamaica for a wonderful honeymoon.

After returning home, they put their noses to the grindstone. They rented a comfortable little furnished apartment because they had no furniture. They both wanted a home of their own, and fortunately with the help of their parents were able to purchase a home six months later.

Their credit was not very good because they had not established a credit history. Dale still owed a large sum on his education.

They gradually furnished their home and looked forward to having children. Time passed as two, three, and finally five years went by and still no children. They both had medical exams and the doctor could not find a medical reason for their infertility. He said, "Maybe you just have not given it enough time or perhaps you are too worried about not having children".

Dale and Nancy wanted to have a family while they were still young. After finishing their educations and after several passing years, the desire to have a family became more urgent. It was a consuming desire that was always in their mind and a constant topic of conversation.

CHAPTER 4

A Change in Location

*D*ale had a good job, but Scott and Associates Law Firm in Cleveland, Ohio, called and requested that he come up for an interview. He had worked on some high priority cases and received much publicity. That had a lot to do with the contact by Scott and Jones for the interview. They asked that he meet with them on Thursday. It was not a problem to take the time off. The president of his current firm happened to know the president of Scott and Jones.

Dale arrived in Cleveland at 1 p.m. on Thursday and was met at the airport by a member of the firm. He showed Dale around the city and later they went to a baseball game. The Cleveland Indians happened to be in town. They had a great evening and after the game, he dropped Dale off at the hotel.

Dale had an appointment at their office at 9 a.m. on Friday. When he arrived at the office, he met several of the attorneys who took him on a tour of the offices. During the interview, the president, John Scott, said that he was impressed with some of the cases that Dale had tried. His expertise had been a major reason for the success of his current employer.

Dale was a little intimidated by the size of the firm and the number of employees. After a lengthy interview and the good impression that he made on Scott and Associates, he was offered the job.

They gave him thirty days in order to give a notice to his current firm, sell his home, and for Nancy to give a notice at the hospital.

They both worked a two-week notice. They put their house on the market and in the meantime made several trips to Cleveland looking for a house. The firm there knew what they were looking for in a house and directed them to a compatible realtor.

Fortunately, they found a house that they both liked. It included some of the things that Nancy really wanted; a large porch and a backyard for the kids that they planned to have later. The yard had some big trees and Dale could picture a swing set under them with a couple of kids swinging. They agreed on this house, and then had to get a contract on their old house. Within a couple of weeks, they had a contract on the house. They also signed a contract on the house in Cleveland.

They began to pack and prepare for the move. They didn't know how long it would take to close out the current house or the one in Cleveland, but felt certain that this was God's plan for them.

CHAPTER 5

Making the Move and Meeting a New Friend

*A*fter the closing on the houses, they rented a moving van and started packing their belongings for Cleveland. They only had one week from the time they worked their two-week notices until Dale started his new job.

Nancy didn't have a job waiting for her. They moved and got their things situated in their new home. In the meantime, Nancy had some time for job hunting. There were several large hospitals in Cleveland and they didn't think it would be a problem finding work as a nurse. Fortunately, she found a job right away.

Nancy was hired for a job that was some distance away, but that was not a problem. She could use their car since they lived on the bus route. Dale could take the bus until they got on their feet and could afford another car.

Dale settled into his job and loved it. Things went well and he liked the people in the firm. They all usually went out to lunch, but Dale didn't care to go out every day. He liked for Nancy to pack his lunch some days, and he would eat in the office. It gave him an opportunity to get some extra work done.

He looked out his office window on one bright sunlit day and saw a park bench near a fence. He decided to go outside and eat his lunch in the sunshine. After that, on several Wednesdays and Fridays, he would eat in the park.

One day during lunch, a baseball came over the fence and landed near him. He looked around to see where it came from, and a voice behind him said, "Hey Mister, would you hand me my ball".

Dale responded, "Certainly".

He got up, retrieved the ball and walked back to the fence to hand it to the youngster. The boy had blue eyes, blonde hair and a winning smile. Dale had the strangest feeling he had ever had. He had never seen the boy before, but remembered someone who looked like him and spoke like him. Dale asked him how old he was.

The boy said, "I'm eight years old".

Dale thought, "He's tall for his age". He didn't understand why he had such strong feelings for this little boy.

Apparently, the way he stared at Dale meant he had similar feelings. Dale told him to back up and he would throw the ball over the fence. The young boy then went on his way as Dale finished his lunch.

Dale went back inside, but a few days later came outside to eat lunch again. The boy came up to the fence and said, "hey Mister "

This time, no baseball had come over the fence.

Dale asked, "What's your name"?

The boy smiled and said, "My name is Johnny".

They talked a while and Dale asked him, "Well, how are you doing, Johnny?"

"I like talking to you, " Johnny answered. "Thanks for giving the ball back the other day. I've got to go now."

Johnny turned and ran.

This happened on a regular basis. He made a habit of coming out to talk to Dale. Some days Dale was out of town, at other times the weather was too bad, or he was too busy. He didn't go out to eat on a regular basis, but noticed one day while sitting in his office eating lunch there was an orphanage behind the fence in the park. That must be where Johnny lived.

Dale looked closer and could see Johnny standing at a window looking toward the park to see if Dale was going to come out to eat. He could see other boys of Johnny's size in the doorways and windows, who must also be residents of the orphanage.

The next day Dale carried his lunch. He thought, "I am going to go out and be there if Johnny comes out today".

He went out, and sure enough, Johnny came to the fence. Dale said hello and after a moment asked, "Why do you come out to the fence every day"?

Johnny said, "I don't know, but I just feel good when I am around you." He smiled shyly when he said this and it melted Dale's heart.

Dale couldn't understand why he was so emotional about this orphan boy, but there was a connection that could not be explained. "I like you, too, Johnny, and enjoy talking with you. Someday, I would like to have a little boy just like you."

As Dale spoke these words, he could sense eagerness in Johnny's expression and a sense of urgency.

Johnny said, "I bet you would be a good dad. Your kids would be lucky." Then his expression became sad. "We don't have dads here. The people treat us okay, but it's not the same."

Johnny hung his head to hide the tears that glistened in his eyes.

This exchange went on for several weeks. Johnny came out and talked to Dale every time he went to the park to eat his lunch. He found out some things about Johnny and his family, and Dale told him about his own family.

Johnny was always inquisitive about Dale's wife and wanted to know if she wanted children.

He told him that he and his wife wanted several children, but had been married for seven and a half years without children.

Johnny asked Dale unexpectedly, "Have you ever thought about adopting children?"

Dale was surprised and said, "We don't want to adopt a child. We want to have our own children. Because we both came from large families, our goal is to have several children."

Johnny kept on talking about adoption. He got so close to Dale, and many of the things he said touched Dale so much, that he could hardly handle it.

Johnny said, "There isn't any thing wrong with adopting a child. If I was adopted, I would help around the house. I could do housework. When you have children, I could help take care of them. I have a little sister who is two and a half years younger than I am, but I don't know where she is now. I helped take care of her."

Johnny continued, "When my mother died in a car wreck, I was seven and a half years old, and I had to take care of my sister because my daddy drank all the time. When they put us in an orphanage I helped take care of her until she went to a foster home. I miss her so much. I really love her. When my mom was alive, she carried us to church every Sunday. She taught me how to pray. I gave my heart to Jesus and became a Christian when I was seven years old."

Johnny swallowed hard as he thought about his sister and said, "I pray for my sister every day, that she will be safe. I will pray for you and your wife, too - that you will have children of your own and have a happy home."

He went on, "I have prayed that God will give us a home, and that my sister and I will have a mom and a dad. I never see my daddy any more. He used to come around on special occasions, but he didn't even come around for my eighth birthday. I don't know where my daddy is anymore.

"I had a small family because my mom and dad eloped and got married and never went back. So, I never knew my grandparents or the rest of my family. I can't help but wonder how nice it would be to belong to a family and have some one to love and some one to love me. That's my goal in life - to have some one to love me and adopt me."

He looked at Dale and said, "I love you".

Dale said, "I love you, too, Johnny, but I can't adopt you. My wife doesn't want to adopt children because we want to have children of our own."

CHAPTER 6

Nancy Objects to Adoption

$\mathcal{D}$ale told Nancy what Johnny said, and she was very upset. "We are not going to adopt a child, no matter what Johnny says to you. Don't pay any attention to him. We're going to live our own lives. Let somebody else adopt him."

Dale told her, "I just wish you would go and meet him. You are off on Friday. "Let's take our lunch and go and sit on the park bench and eat lunch together. The weather is supposed to be pretty Friday, and we'll see if Johnny comes out to talk to you."

Nancy got there a little bit early and Dale had a feeling that Johnny was watching. It turned out that he was. Dale knew that Johnny only had thirty minutes to wash his hands, eat lunch, play a little, and be back in class. He came out as soon as Dale and Nancy got there at noon.

Knowing that he only had a limited time to eat Dale asked, "What will you do about lunch?"

Johnny said, "Oh, it doesn't matter about eating lunch. I just wanted to come out and meet your wife."

Dale had told him that he might bring her some time and have her eat lunch with them.

Dale said, "Johnny, you come out here and don't even eat your lunch. You're a growing boy and need to eat."

He smiled and said, "I had rather be out here with you both than to eat my lunch anyway."

So they talked awhile and Johnny asked Nancy some questions. She had some questions for him as well.

Johnny looked up at the couple and said, "I bet you two would make wonderful parents".

Nancy had a frozen look on her face. She said, Well, we have to go," and turned abruptly and walked away. After telling Johnny goodbye, Dale caught up with her.

"I wish I had never agreed to come." It was easy for Dale to see how upset she was, but over the next few days, it weighed heavily on her mind.

CHAPTER 7

God Begins to Touch Nancy's Heart

Each day, Dale would tell her things Johnny had said. At one point, she didn't even want Dale to eat lunch outside and see Johnny any more. Dale didn't think there was any harm in that, however, and continued to see Johnny almost every day that he was in town.

A couple of months later, Nancy said, "I'd like to eat lunch with you on Friday and see Johnny again."

Dale was shocked. He knew she hadn't changed her mind about adopting children. She wanted to carry, to give birth to, and to raise her own child.

Johnny was there to meet both of them as soon as his class was over. Dale told him he needed to eat his lunch first.

Johnny told Dale, "That doesn't matter. I'd rather be around you two than eat my lunch. I can eat my lunch later."

They had a long visit that day. Dale had him to tell Nancy some of the things that he had told him about his mother and sister. Johnny repeated how she was killed in a car wreck when he was seven and a half years old, and told Nancy about his life at the orphanage. He had been carried out a couple of times to foster homes. He said it was very lonely there with no family after his sister went to live in different foster homes.

Adoption was hard and rare, especially for boys Johnny's age. He could sense when people really liked him. He told Dale later, "I know you love me. I can tell you love me and I love you."

It broke Dale's heart when he talked like that. They had a nice long visit that day, but Dale didn't know what to do about his situation. He found himself praying that someone would adopt Johnny and give him a good home.

He had continued to go outside to eat lunch, but he hadn't seen Johnny in awhile. He wondered if he had been placed in a foster home.

Dale watched for Johnny for a long time after that. He went out several times to eat and Johnny didn't show up. He watched from the window and didn't see him any more. About four weeks passed and still no Johnny.

Dale told Nancy about his concern. She said, "Well, go over to the orphanage and find out if anything wrong".

Dale replied, "I'll go when I get off work this afternoon". When he arrived, he was told that Johnny was extremely sick and in the hospital. They were not sure what was wrong with him. Dale asked if it would be all right if he went to see him. The lady asked if Dale was the man who ate lunch in the park.

"Yes, I'm the one."

The lady said,"Johnny enjoys coming out to the fence and talking to you, and thinks the world of you."

CHAPTER 8

Johnny Has a Crisis

Dale went to the hospital to visit Johnny, who was very sick and running a high fever. The medical staff was giving him several medications and was undecided what to do next. Johnny was not responding to the medication. When Dale approached his bed and picked up Johnny's feverish hand, Johnny squeezed his hand weakly. He didn't speak, but Dale could tell that Johnny knew he was there for him. The doctor told Dale that Johnny's kidneys weren't functioning properly. It was a dangerous situation.

Dale asked if there was anything he could do. The doctor said that there was nothing to do but pray for Johnny. It was comforting to Dale to know that Johnny's doctor believed in prayer. He knew that doctors can be tools of God in healing the sick.

Dale was a lawyer and not a doctor. He felt helpless as he watched the pale, weak boy toss fitfully as he suffered from his illness. The doctor asked if Dale was a relative.

Dale said, "No, just a close friend, but it hurts to see him suffer like that."

The doctor said, "We must find out what is wrong. He's growing weaker and we could lose him soon."

They decided to put him on a dialysis machine and that helped tremendously. They determined that his problem was with his kidneys. They were not functioning properly, not purifying his blood. They needed to give him blood and needed blood donors, and possibly a donor for a kidney transplant. Finding his real family was critical, but they had been unsuccessful so far in doing that.

CHAPTER 9

The Search for Johnny's Family

$\mathcal{D}$ale was a lawyer and knew detectives who would know how to find Johnny' family. He got a couple of colleagues from his firm to work on the case as well, to see what they could find out. They were glad to help and started working the case immediately. They would get back in touch with Dale as things developed.

They soon found Frank Moore, Johnny's father, who told them the same story that Johnny had told Dale and Nancy about Johnny's mother being killed in a car wreck. They told him that Johnny was in the hospital and deathly sick. Johnny's father was homeless, no job and an alcoholic. He did say that he would come to the hospital to see Johnny.

Mr. Moore was asked to donate a sample of his blood to see if he could be a blood donor for Johnny. He was also asked if he would be tested to see if he could possibly donate a kidney, if Johnny needed it. When the blood test came back, they found out that he was not a candidate for blood donations or as a kidney donor. The doctors said they would have to find someone else as a candidate - very soon.

"We may have to do exploratory surgery to find out the exact cause of the problem," they said. "If we don't find someone to give him a kidney, he will be on dialysis the rest of his life. You don't want anyone, especially a young boy, to have to live that way if it can be avoided."

Dale heard all this and it troubled him deeply. "Even though I hardly know the boy," he thought, " he is a human being and a good boy, and if there is anything I can do I am going to do it. Maybe I could be a blood donor, or maybe even give him a kidney."

Dale told the doctors he would have to talk it over with his wife. He would have to see if he qualified as a blood and kidney donor by having tests of his own blood. In the meantime, they would try to learn more from the father, but the detectives found him very reluctant to give much information. Dale had gotten more information from Johnny than they got from his father.

They needed to know who the mother was before she married. They did finally manage to get a copy of the marriage license and learned her maiden name. They found information about her family, but her mother and father were deceased. When she married, she left home and never went back, so the extended family knew nothing about the children. They never had a chance to adopt the children because the father had not contacted them.

Nancy went to the hospital to see Johnny, and it seemed as if she suddenly fell in love with him. The situation made her sorry for him and aroused her maternal instincts. She wanted Dale to do whatever he could to help the boy.

At that point, Dale knew if Johnny needed a kidney and he was compatible, he was going to give it to him. A DNA test was performed on the father and also on Dale to see if he could give Johnny a kidney. Nancy and Dale decided that Johnny was going to need some special attention for a while, even if he got the kidney, and decided to see if they could be foster parents to Johnny and take care of him. They both knew they loved him and hoped that perhaps someday they could adopt him.

CHAPTER 10

Johnny's True Identity Revealed

*D*ale and Nancy started checking out the possibility of being foster parents and adopting Johnny. They scheduled a meeting before the judge. They met in the judges chambers. Mr. Moore was there with his lawyer. Dale and Nancy had their own attorney there, to file a petition before the court for them to be foster parents or adopt Johnny.

They knew Johnny was very sick and was going to need a lot of special care. Since Nancy was a nurse they felt that this would be the best way to be sure that he received the proper care. Mr. Moore said that he would not sign any adoptions papers. He said, "I have lost track of my daughter, and I am not going to lose my son."

The judge asked him, "How do you propose to take care of your son? The court has already ruled you an unfit parent."

Then he said, " I'll sign the papers for $50,000."

There was a knock on the door and the judge's secretary asked permission for the technician from the lab to enter the judges chambers. The judge asked if this pertained to the case at hand, and the secretary replied that it did. The technician entered and asked if he could speak. He has been working with Dale to find someone who could donate blood or a kidney to Johnny.

The technician said, "Through DNA we found out that Mr. Moore is not Johnny's father."

Mr. Moore became extremely agitated and the judge had to demand that he be seated and be quiet.

Moore said, "I am Johnny's father, and I am going to get another lawyer and sue all of you." He stormed out of the judge's chambers.

The judge asked the technician if that was all. He said, "No sir. I have some additional information. We know who the father of Johnny is. The judge asked, Who is the actual father?"

The technician said, "Dale Goodman is the father, and he doesn't have to adopt Johnny because he is already his son."

Dale said, "How in the world could I be his father?"

"The DNA proves that you are the father."

Dale asked the technician if he knew Johnny's mothers maiden name. When he told Dale the name, he knew it was his first wife. Soon after their brief marriage, her father had the marriage annulled. He didn't know that she was pregnant because he never heard from her again.

Johnny had told Dale that his mom and dad had eloped and gotten married. So apparently, she and her ex-boyfriend eloped and got married immediately and she didn't tell him that she was pregnant.

CHAPTER 11

Good News and a Successful Surgery

Everyone agreed to keep this information about Johnny's true identity confidential, and the judge agreed. Nancy spoke to the judge, "Your honor, I would like to adopt Johnny."

With authorization from the judge, plans were for Nancy and Dale to adopt Johnny. The judge said that he would get in touch with the orphanage and let them know the arrangements, and when Johnny was able, they could take him to their home.

Dale and Nancy decided not to tell Johnny yet that Dale was his real father. He was not old enough to understand.

They planned to go back to the hospital and Nancy and Dale would be with him next day if they performed surgery. They decided not to tell him about the adoption now. They would wait until he got through this and felt better before they told him.

They went back to the hospital and saw the doctor. He said, "I have some good news. We have run more tests, and we think Johnny has a growth or tumor that is blocking the blood flow to his kidneys. That is the reason his kidneys are not purifying his blood. We will do exploratory surgery in the morning. If what we think is true and we remove the blockage, we think Johnny's kidneys will be fine."

Dale and Nancy were overjoyed, praising God for his blessings. They stayed with Johnny for a while. The doctor said they couldn't do anything for him that night, and for them to go home, get some rest and come back in the morning to see him before surgery.

He said, "We don't think the surgery will last but two and a half or three hours.

The doctor came out of the operating room about two and a half hours after the surgery began and told Dale and Nancy, "Everything went well. Johnny is going to be fine. He is a strong young man and should recover quickly."

Dale and Nancy were allowed to go in and see Johnny. Back in his room, he was still groggy, but he managed to give them a smile. He knew who they were and he squeezed Dale's hand.

Johnny enjoyed all the attention that he was getting. They didn't mention anything about his identity yet. They were going to wait a few days. The doctor came in and said he could go home in two or three days. Dale asked him if he would like to go home with him and Nancy and let them take care of him until he got well.

Johnny was overjoyed. It made him so animated that Dale was afraid he would hurt himself. Dale thought, "Maybe that will make him get well even faster because he sure does want to go home with us."

Dale told Johnny, "I will carry you home with us if you will call me dad instead of mister."

Somehow, Dale thought Johnny fell in love with them even before they did him. Dale told Johnny, "We are going to be your foster parents and someday maybe your real parents."

Johnny said. "Dad, you know I love you".

That was the first time anyone had called him dad, and Dale said, "Johnny, I love you too."

He was so excited and he didn't know what to do about having a mom and dad who loved him. "I prayed for a long time for this to happen," Johnny said. "Dad, I am ready to go home."

Dale said, "Johnny, you can't go home for a day or so until the doctor dismisses you from the hospital."

Dale thought how he and Nancy prayed for children and didn't know that God would open up a door like this. They loved Johnny very much, but still prayed for children of their own. What made it so wonderful was that Johnny was also praying for them to have children. He told Dale once that if they had children, he could help take care of them.

Dale told Johnny that they had to go and he didn't want them to leave. Dale told him that they had to go buy him a bed.

Johnny laughed and said, "It's all right if you go. But, I can sleep on anything."

Dale told him, "I am going to fix you a nice room."

"O.K." Johnny replied, "but let me hug you before you go."

"We will be back in the morning," Dale promised. "Right now, I've got to move all my office furniture and make you a bedroom out of my office."

CHAPTER 12

Johnny has a Real Home

$\mathcal{D}$ale and Nancy purchased a bedroom suite, which would be delivered the next day. They would have to work late into the night to clean out the room. Dale called the orphanage and told them he would come by the next day and pick up Johnny's clothes and personal belongings.

The people at the orphanage were excited that Johnny would have a good foster home, because they knew that Johnny loved Dale very much. Dale picked up Johnny's clothes and went back by the hospital. Nancy was already there. They were both very excited because the doctor had said Johnny could go home the next day.

Dale and Nancy's pastor had visited Johnny that day. Johnny was happy to see him. He told him, "Preacher, I will be coming to your church now because I am going home with Dale and Nancy." Johnny asked the preacher to pray for him, and to also pray that Nancy and Dale would someday have children of their own.

They brought Johnny to his new home, and he was so glad to have a mom and dad. He said, "I have prayed for this day for a long time." He was so tickled to see the house, the big porch, and back yard where he could play. He was happy to have a room of his own. He had never had a room of his own. They told him as soon as he felt better, they would take him shopping for clothes and other things for his room.

Johnny said, "I am happy with things just like they are."

Nancy took a leave of absence to stay home and care for Johnny during his recovery. Dale had never seen two people any happier than Nancy and Johnny.

It was almost time for Johnny to start to school, and they enrolled him in a new school. All his paper work would have to be transferred so they decided to leave his name as Johnny Moore until his birth certificate paper work changed.

Now Johnny was back in school and Nancy at her work, but she returned home by the time Johnny arrived from school each day. It was so nice to come home in the afternoon and have someone to greet him and have time to do so many things that he had never had the opportunity to do. Johnny had many memories of his mother and Nancy seemed to fill the need for a mother. They got along so well.

Johnny missed his sister, though - and so much more because he had helped take care of here.

It was late October, and Johnny's birthday was coming in November. Dale asked Johnny what he would like for his birthday.

He said, "I already have everything. The only thing I can think of is that I would like to know that my sister Rachel is okay. She can't do so many things for herself. I would be happy to know that she is happy in her foster home. That's all I would want for my birthday."

Dale told Johnny that he would talk to the people at the orphanage and try to find out where Rachel was.

"I don't know how long it will take, and its just three weeks until your birthday. But maybe I can find out something by then," Dale told him.

Within two days Dale had found out where Rachel was located. He also learned that since they had Johnny, her brother, it would be possible for them to get Rachel for a one-day visit.

It just happened that Johnny's birthday was on Saturday and that would give them time to plan a party. They didn't tell Johnny that they planned to pick up Rachel for the day. They wanted it to be a surprise. They told Johnny he could invite some of his friends from his Sunday school class.

Johnny would be nine years old and this would be his first birthday party. He said, "I have been having a party for the last three months, and I am the happiest that I have ever been. It's so good to have a mom and dad that I love and they love me".

CHAPTER 13

Johnny makes a Wish

$\mathcal{D}$ale continued to make contact with the orphanage and found out what time he could pick Rachel up the day of the party and what time he needed to have her back. They continued to make plans for the party. They bought Johnny some toys as well as gifts for Rachel, although they had to hide them from Johnny because it was going to be a surprise that Rachel would be coming to the party.

When Johnny said his prayers at night, he always prayed that Rachel was all right and being cared for properly.

Dale and Nancy felt so blessed to have Johnny in their home. He really enjoyed going to church and made many friends there.

This was the big day! It was Johnny's ninth birthday and his first party! The weather was cool but the sun was shining, so Dale hoped that the boys would be able to go outside and play for a while.

The party would begin at 2 p.m., but Dale would be picking up Rachel at 9 that morning because he wanted them to have some time together before his friends arrived.

When he picked up Rachel, she was so excited about seeing Johnny. She was poorly dressed, but a beautiful little girl. Dale told her that Johnny didn't know that she was coming and would be very surprised. She spoke up and said, "I love Johnny. I would love to have a birthday party sometime, too."

Dale said, "Well, maybe some day soon you will have a party."

They arrived back at the house and from where they parked, Johnny wasn't able to see the car. He carried Rachel to the front door and let her ring the bell because he knew Johnny would answer the door. When he opened the door and saw Rachel, they both screamed and hugged each other. Then Johnny came over and thanked Dale for bringing Rachel to the party. He was so glad to see her. "How long can she stay?" he asked Dale.

Dale told him, "All day until 5 p.m. That's when I need to have her back."

Dale had never seen two children that age who cared for each other as much as Johnny and Rachel. Each one wanted to know what the other one had been doing. Johnny really wanted to know if Rachel was being taken care of and if she was happy where she was.

She said, "They take good care of me, but I want to live with you."

They hardly got out of each others sight all day. They held hands and played together more than he played with his friends who came to the party. Dale could already see that he was going to have a hard time separating the two of them.

Johnny enjoyed the party and was so grateful for his gifts. He thanked all his friends for coming to his party. After everyone had left, Dale and Nancy enjoyed sitting around and watching the two children play together. Time was drawing near for Rachel to leave, so Dale told her to get her gifts together.

She and Johnny held each other, cried, and said "NO, NO, NO".

Johnny said, "If you will let her stay I will take care of her. She can have my room, and I will sleep on the floor.

"No, Johnny, that was the agreement we had with the orphanage, that I would only have her for the day," Dale said.

Johnny said, "Please let her stay another hour".

Dale said, "No Johnny. I can't do that, but I promise that you will get to see her again before long."

They kept hugging each other and Dale finally got them separated. He carried Rachel out the door crying, and left Johnny with Nancy crying. He promised himself if there was anything he could do to arrange for them to live together, he would.

CHAPTER 14

Christmas Preparations

*W*hen Dale and Rachel returned to the orphanage, he talked to the officials and discovered that the foster family where Rachel was living had several other children and were willing to let Rachel go to live with someone else. Dale told them that he would discuss this with Nancy, but thought it would be good if the brother and sister could be re-united and live together. They informed him that the contract with the foster family ran out in December, and Dale said that he thought they would like to take Rachel into their home.

Dale returned home, helped Nancy clean up the mess from the party, and got Johnny ready for bed. When Johnny prayed that night, he prayed for Rachel and the other kids still at the orphanage. He also said that in his prayer that he was thankful for his new mom and dad.

After they put Johnny to bed, Nancy and Dale went back to the den and talked for a while. Dale said, "I know that you love Johnny, but I would like to know how you feel about Rachel. How would you feel about being a foster parent to Rachel? I saw the love in your eyes. I know that you care for both of them."

She responded, "I could love both of them, but I still want children of our own, too. It felt like a family today. The laughter and tears of the children made it feel like a home. If Rachel comes to stay with us, we will need another bedroom."

Dale said, "I don't know if it would be possible for us to get Rachel, and we don't want to say anything to Johnny right now because we wouldn't want to disappoint him if it didn't work out. It's a month to Christmas and we are going to start now to plan for a big Christmas. We're going to the have the biggest Christmas ever. We have always gone back to Greensboro to have Christmas with our families. We didn't decorate the house or have a tree because we were not home for Christmas. But this year, since we have Johnny and hope to have Rachel, we should have Christmas at home. We can decorate the house, have a large tree, and have a lot of homemade goodies for the kids. After Christmas, we can go home to Greensboro for a visit. "

Dale told Nancy that he would work with the orphanage and try to have Rachel home with them by Christmas. He requested that he could get Rachel on December 18, since that would begin the school break for the holidays. They wanted her then so she could help Johnny and the family decorate for Christmas. If everything worked out, Rachel would be in a new school after the holidays, which would be a good time for a change. She would be in the same school as Johnny, which would be great.

The next project for Dale and Nancy was to fix up another bedroom for Rachel. It was a busy time preparing for the new arrival, shopping for Christmas and buying toys for the kids. It was a treat for Dale and Nancy to buy toys for a boy and a girl.

Johnny didn't know, but they were not going to get a tree until Rachel arrived so that she could help decorate it.

Dale and Nancy were as excited as kids themselves as they tried to make life better for Johnny and Rachel.

December 18th suddenly arrived. It seemed that time flew by with a child in the house and the extra responsibility that it involved. There was much more work to prepare for Christmas that they were not accustomed to since Johnny was living with them. Nancy was exhausted, but was very excited.

Dale went to pick up Rachel. When they arrived back home, he didn't let her go in the house with him. He went in and asked Johnny if he would like Rachel to come and live with them.

Johnny shouted, "It would be the greatest thing that ever happened to me." He grabbed Dale, hugged him, and cried. "I would give anything for Rachel to come and live with us. I would take care of her."

Dale said, "Would you like for her to come today?"

Through his tears, Johnny said, "I would. I have prayed for a long time that this day would come."

Dale said, "Well, hold my hand," and he walked with Johnny to the door.

Dale opened the door and Rachel ran into the room. She and Johnny hugged and cried and Johnny said, "Now we can be a family again. I have wanted this for a long time and knew that God could do it, but didn't know how it would happen."

They had such a good time playing that lunch arrived before they knew it. Nancy had prepared some special treats especially for the kids.

The weather had turned bad and there was snow in the area, so they decided to wait until the next day to go out for a tree. They spent the rest of the afternoon playing with the kids and putting the final touches on Rachel's room.

Rachel was very excited about having a room of her own. They discovered that she had very few clothes when they were putting them away in her room. Her pajamas were worn and almost too small for her. They promised her that they would buy her some new clothes before school started again.

It was getting late. Dale suggested that it was time for Johnny and Rachel to get ready for bed. Nancy said she would help Rachel shampoo her hair. Rachel said she wasn't used to having help with her bath and enjoyed Nancy's shampooing her hair. She had pretty, blond hair, with natural curl, but it needed a trim at the beauty salon.

When she put on her pajamas, they told her that they would carry her tomorrow and buy her some new ones. She responded, "I'm not used to having anyone make a fuss over me."

After bath time, everyone went back into the den and the kids play together for a while. They were still so excited that it seemed they might not sleep at all that night. After a while, they had snack time and then gathered in the den for family prayers.

Dale took Johnny while Nancy took Rachel to their rooms. Dale was afraid that Johnny would not sleep for fear that Rachel would not be there in the morning. Dale had never seen two children love each other so much. Johnny was only nine years old, but very mature for his age. He was so protective of Rachel.

Nancy and Dale sat in the den after the children were in bed and talked for a while. They talked about the fact that they had never planned to adopt children, but they agreed that when you pray for children, God can answer your prayers in different ways.

Dale had no idea that anybody could fall in love with children so fast. They still wanted children of their own, but were so thankful that God allowed Johnny and Rachel to come into their lives. They vowed to work hard to adopt them and keep them together.

It was bedtime for the adults as well. It was so much busier with the kids around and they seemed to get tired earlier.

The next morning, Johnny and Rachel were up early and excited about going to get a Christmas tree, even though there was still snow on the ground. Maybe they were more eager because of that.

They had some decorations, but not enough for the large tree they picked out, so they went out again for more decorations. Johnny said, "This is going to be fantastic." He could hardly contain himself.

They finished decorating the tree and Nancy decided that she and Rachel would go shopping for clothes and some more gifts. She said, "Why don't you take Johnny shopping? Don't plan on supper together since we will be late.

It was late when we all returned home from our separate shopping trips. The kids were very excited since they had selected gifts for each other. It had been a busy day, so the kids were soon in bed.

Afterwards, Dale and Nancy busily wrapped gifts and placed them under the tree. They were as tired as the children and soon went to bed.

The next day, they were up early and started their day. It was good to see the excitement of the kids being together for Christmas. Johnny was a ball of fire and wanted to decorate the windows and the outside of the house. So did Rachel. Excited, he told Dale and Nancy, "the greatest thing about Christmas is having a family and all being together."

Christmas was just around the corner and Nancy still had much to do - address cards, shop, cook, and bake more goodies for the family. Dale decided to take the kids out for the day and give her some personal time for some of the chores. While they were out, they would buy Nancy gifts from Johnny and Rachel.

When they returned home, the house smelled wonderful, with all the scents and aromas of Christmas. They could smell cinnamon, spices, the scent of the live tree and it spurred their excitement to a fever pitch. Nancy had been baking and the house was filled with the allure of all the special treats that she had prepared.

Rachel and Johnny were curious about the large stack of gifts under the tree and wanted to shake them all. Dale told them, "That is a no, no!" but they danced around the tree, knocking off ornaments and replacing them until bedtime. They were told that it was time for baths and bed.

After baths, they gathered in the den for prayer time. Dale asked Johnny if he would like to lead the prayer and Johnny said, "Yes, I would."

He prayed, "Lord, thank you for what you have done for Rachel and me, and for giving us a new home. Bless the children at the orphanage and help them find a home, too. Help the homeless people to have food and a place to sleep. Thank you for our new mom and dad and bless them with children of their own. Help Rachel and me to be good because our new mom and dad love us so much."

CHAPTER 15

A Christmas Miracle

*C*hristmas Eve arrived and they needed to get the kids to bed early so that Santa Claus could come. Nancy put Rachel to bed and Dale took care of Johnny. They went back to the den to make the final preparations for Santa's visit. They were so happy to see the children's excitement. This was their first Christmas having a part in choosing the tree, decorating and buying gifts for each other. They finished the preparations about midnight and went to bed tired, but happy.

Dale had told them to leave milk and cookies for Santa Claus.

Johnny woke Dale up early the next morning, shaking him and telling him that Santa had come "because he drank the milk and ate the cookies". He ran to wake up Rachel and they hurried together to the tree, saw all the gifts, and called for Nancy and Dale to come and see.

They opened packages and had lots of toys and pretty clothes. They also each had a shiny new bike. They played with the new toys all day. Some of Johnny's games were too mature for Rachel, so Dale played games with Johnny and Nancy played dolls and "dress-up" with Rachel's pretty new doll and doll clothes. They took a break for lunch and were soon back to play. The kids were very tired by nightfall and went to bed early.

The 26th was spent packing and preparing for the trip to Greensboro the next day. The drive would be long, so they left early. They arrived late in the afternoon. They went to Dale's parents home first, and they gave the children a warm welcome. Johnny never met a stranger, but Rachel was a little shy. Plans were to spend the night and have Christmas there for the kids.

The 28th was spent with Nancy's parents and it was a wonderful holiday celebrating Christmas and the fact that they had been blessed with the addition of Johnny and Rachel to their family.

It was a wonderful visit with both families and Dale and Nancy were so pleased at how the families had accepted the children.

Johnny and Rachel were happy to have new grandparents and delighted in all the extra gifts showered on them. They planned to return the next day and Dale wondered how he would get all of the gifts into the car for the return to Cleveland.

Rachel was scheduled to enter her new school soon and Johnny would be going back to school as well.
Nancy had a doctor's appointment for a check-up. She was not feeling well. She and Dale suspected that it was the exhaustion from all the extra work preparing for Christmas. She has been working harder with two children in the house and the stress of Christmas had taken its toll. Dale thought that Nancy probably just needs some rest, and maybe some vitamins.

They enjoyed being home and Nancy got Rachel enrolled at school as Dale kept Johnny at home. After they returned, Nancy went for her doctor's appointment.

Dale was sitting in the floor playing with the kids when Nancy returned. As she entered the room, Dale could see that something was wrong. Nancy was laughing and crying at the same time.

Dale jumped to his feet, "What's wrong?"

Johnny and Rachel gathered around her with concern as Dale waited for her response.

Nancy said, "Nothing is wrong. Everything is right. We are going to have a baby."

Johnny hugged them both as Dale and Nancy hugged each other. He said, "I knew God would answer our prayers."

Rachel began to cry and asked, "Since you are going to have a baby, will you still let me live here?"

Dale and Nancy hugged her, kissed her, and told her that they were her foster parents. They were planning to adopt both of them.

Dale said, "You are part of our family and will always have a home with us. We feel that both of you have been a "Godsend". You made our house a home and our family complete. Regardless of how many children we have, you will always be our special children too.

EPILOGUE

God worked through Dale and Nancy's love to bring them together with Johnny and Rachel. God revealed Dale's father/son relationship with Johnny and allowed him to make Johnny a permanent part of his and Nancy's lives.

Because of the love that Dale and Nancy showed for these children, God chose to bless them with another child of their own.

God's love knows no boundaries. Nothing is impossible for Him.

LaVergne, TN USA
07 April 2010
178539LV00001B/18/P